CRYSTAL HEALING

Heal Yourself

Gene Meyer

10-10-10
Publishing

CRYSTAL HEALING
www.crystalhealingtoday.com
Copyright © 2021 Gene Meyer

Paperback ISBN: 978-1-77277-454-2

Publisher
10-10-10 Publishing
Markham, ON   Canada

Printed in Canada and the United States of America

Table of Contents

This book is dedicated to Marcel Vogel, who first taught me how to use his Vogel crystals and the many healing techniques associated with helping the sick.

Acknowledgements

Special thanks to my family and friends who have always been there to support me over the years.

A special thank you to Mark DeMarco for editing, proof-reading, and formatting.

Super thanks to Raymond Aaron for making this book possible.

About the Author

Gene Meyer is a successful Canadian business person, owning his own insurance company in Mississauga for many years. He comes to us from Germany, where he was born, by way of Montreal. Gene has lived in the greater Toronto area since 1968.

Foreword

Do you want to change your life for the better? Are you interested in learning about the healing power of crystals? If so, then this is the book for you!

Author Gene Meyer first learned about crystals in 1978, and has been working with them in a healing capacity since the early eighties. His purpose in writing this book is to provide you with explicit step-by-step instructions for self-healing, and to explain the mystical healing powers of crystals.

After receiving positive feedback from around the globe about the healings he performed, he wishes to pass along these same healing methods to you. Through this book, you too can open your mind, heart, and sensitivity to the remarkable energies of healing crystals.

If you are looking to heal yourself, this book is for you. You will discover that crystals are much more than a fashion accessory. Join Gene on this incredibly rewarding journey today, and learn how crystals can change your life!

Raymond Aaron
New York Times **Bestselling Author**

Chapter 1

What is a Vogel Healing Crystal?

Where Do We Find the Raw Quartz Crystal?

Clear Quartz is known as the "Master Healer" because it is the most powerful healer with its very high vibration, and is the most versatile healing stone among all crystals. Clear Quartz is also known as the "Stone of Power" and amplifies any energy or intention. It is believed to protect against negativity, and attune to your higher self. Quartz crystals are very programmable and tend to hold a program much longer than other minerals. The totally clear crystals are unearthed in Brazil, the Himalayas, the US, and China. You can purchase them at gem shops or Amazon-Etsy and other mail order companies.

Who Does the Cutting?

There is a master cutter trained by Marcel Vogel Drew Tousley at Luminary Studios in California. Also, Ray Pinto is in Brazil. He cuts large crystals up to 11 inches long and up to almost 400 sides totally clear. Ray owns several mines, and flies in with a helicopter to collect them. The clear big ones are from Samco South American Mining Corporation. There are many more that cut crystals around the globe.

How Many Cuts or Sides Should Your Crystal Have?

When you purchase your first crystal you should start with a six sided crystal, that fits into your palm. It should be 3.00 inches to 5.5 inches long—not longer. Training with a small crystal that fits into your palm is best. The base is the thick part that should go into your palm. The top pointed part will be manipulated with your index finger to produce the energy to be used on yourself or a person in need.

Should It Be Clear?

The best energy flow comes from a totally clear quartz crystal. Quartz crystals come in many shapes and sizes. I am using specially cut Marcel Vogel Crystals. Marcel was my teacher. He was a scientist at IBM. When Marcel retired, he started training people how to use his cut crystals. The chemical composition: Quartz is a crystalline form of silica — silicon dioxide, SiO_2.

How is the Energy Transferred?

Healing with love. Love is the most powerful energy in our existence, focusing your energy through the crystal into the thymus gland, using pure love. Examples of this are if you hug a little baby, you automatically produce love, or if you take a little cat and hug it you will produce love, or better yet, you must have been in love with someone — do you remember how that felt?

How Do You Remove Old Energies From the Crystal?

The best and simple way I know of is holding your crystal in your left or right hand, completely covering it with your hand if you can, then using intention to clear it, you close your mouth, inhale, concentrate with the intention to clear, and forcefully push the breath out of your nose. You should have a strong magnet one inch away from the crystal, covering all areas to remove the last energy particle from it.

Chapter 2

How Does Healing With a Crystal Work?

Clearing and Charging the Crystal

As stated in the last chapter, you clear a crystal by pulsing your breath with the intention to clear. Once done, you need to charge the crystal with the intention to create lots of love. Again, use your breath and pulse, and imagine love will fill it.

How Long Should Your Crystal Be To Fit Your Hand?

Please do not use larger than 5.5 inches. The giant crystal is only used by master healers and you would need to use both hands because of its weight.

Clearing Old Energies On the Outside First

Use a soft cloth to remove the deposit from your hands.

Specific Rotation To Merge the Energy With Your Body

You place the crystal in your right or left hand pointing towards your thymus gland, where it should sit behind the middle of your breastbone. Put your finger in the indentation beneath about an inch and half —that bone is over your thymus gland.

Point your crystal to the thymus, rotate in small circles five times to the left and five times to the right, then use your intention holding the crystal, close your mouth and carry out a powerful exhale through the nose while you concentrate on releasing your intention.

Termperature Should Be the Same as Your Hand

For the energy transfer and linking with your crystal in your hand, left or right, rotate inward until it gets so sticky that it will stick to your hand—then it is perfect to heal yourself.

Charging With Intent and Love

Take your crystal in either hand covered fully, as mentioned before, closing your eyes. Concentrate on the crystal, create love and shoot it into the crystal with intent to do a great healing on yourself.

Chapter 3

What Kind of Crystal Should I Use For Myself?

Clear Quartz is Best for Healing

Clear quartz is best for healing yourself, but you may also use amethyst, citrine, topaz, calcite or kunzite providing, it has the proper shape.

How Many Sides Should It Have?

For self-healing a six sided or eight sided crystal is best 3, 5.5 inches long.

How Long Should Your Crystal Be?

When you place the crystal in your palm you should be able to manipulate the top with your index finger. The best length is between 3 and 5 inches.

Measuring the Effect of the Crystal On Your Body

Get various samples of stones. You can purchase them in a very nice kit from Amazon or crystal shops in your neighborhood. Close your eyes and extend your arm, put a slight downward pressure on your arm so that the basic resistance or strengthening can be determined. Have someone press on the arm with the crystal and you try to resist your arm from going down with the pressure, then you can experience how good it will work with you and on you.

Also, you can take your crystal and place it on the witness area, three fingers below the low point at the base of the throat. You then ask yourself a question — Is this stone good for me to wear?

Measuing the Power Emanating From a Crystal

Following are the instructions for measuring the power emanating from a crystal versus a Vogel cut crystal or regular cut crystal.

Materials required:

- One large clean Mason type jar with a lid

- Silk thread— large diameter mechanical pencil lead marking pen and nail polish.

- A cut healing crystal and a natural quartz crystal and a tape. Diamagnetic materials are very sensitive to the fields emanating from both determinations of natural crystals in the finished ends of a healing crystal.

A very nice apparatus can be made to measure these fields by taking a large diameter mechanical pencil or lead pencil, or removing the covering of wood from the pencil and cutting a piece of lead about 2 1/2 inches long. Sharpen one end of the lead to a fine point and tie a piece of thread at the middle balance point and brackets of the lid so it hangs horizontally.

Instructions:

- Punch a hole in the center of the jar or lid

- Pass the thread through this hole so that the lead is suspended in the center of the jar and tape the thread to the lid

- On the jar inscribe a series of vertical lines with a permanent marking pen or fingernail polish about an inch apart all around the jar loosely

- See the lid threads on the jar and allow the system to come to balance

- Carefully rotate the lid until the lid points are one of the lines

- To measure the effect of the crystal on the lid, place your left hand on the side of the jar facing the blunt end of the lead with your right hand hold one of the crystals and focus on the sharpened tip of the lead

- Hold the crystal steady, slowly breathe in and out—do this three times

- Watch what's taking place when the lead moves

- Notice and record the deflection

- Reverse the directions of the Crystal

- Repeat the procedure and what was taking place

- One side will deflect in the left-handed direction, the other side will reverse the direction

- Now try it with the other quartz crystal and again record the degree of deflection

- You can now apply where Crystal motion is to the device, then up-and-down the right and left-handed rotation of the crystal

This is a practical and inexpensive tool to measure the crystal's capacity for charge transfer. It is to be tried before and after meals, morning and afternoon, daily at the same time through the five days of a full moon cycle. The physical body is most affected at this time.

The Correct Angles for a Healing Crystal

See diagram for correct healing angles

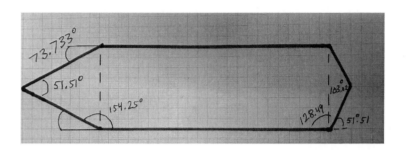

Chapter 4

Techniques for Self-Healing (Part 1)

Insomnia

You can use crystals from mother the earth to fix insomnia so that you can sleep uninterrupted all night long.

Amethyst, Sodalite and Smoky Quartz will help to stop your mind clutter and chatter. Put all three on to your witness area.

Carpal Tunnel

You can reduce the pain by holding the crystal for at least 30 minutes to the hurting wrist. You will need Blue Lace Agate or Fuchsite. Then, after 10 minutes you should massage the area with the crystal.

If You Have Allergies

Please obtain Carnelian and Aquamarine. They will help with hay fever as well. Carry them on you, in what you wear, or you can even wear them as a pendant.

For the Common Cold

Obtain a Jet crystal such as Carnelian, Fluorite and or Moss Agate. You can carry or wear them. You may also create a crystal elixir in your water bottle with these crystals to get rid of a common cold.

Crystals to Reduce Your Asthma

Please wear or carry Tiger Eye (any color), Amber, Morganite or Malachite near your chest. They will reduce and relieve asthma symptoms

Would You Like to Get Rid of Your Headaches?

Place Sugilite and Amethyst crystals, and Peppermint or Lavender essential oils on your forehead for help.

Chapter 5

Techniques for Self-Healing (Part 2)

Crystals for Depression

Wear continually and hold the following crystals on your solar Plexus or your heart chakra: Lapis Lazuli, Jet Crystal, or Smoky Quartz. You can also use Chamomile essential oil.

If You or Someone is Bi-Polar

Charoite, Kunzite, Lepidic or Charoite will assist in managing bi-polar problems. Wear or carry them on you. Also use your favored crystal and place it on your third eye when you meditate.

Crystals for OCD

Use Amethyst, Peridot or Charoite to help with obsessive compulsive disorder. Carry them with you and place on your solar plexus and third eye for 15 minutes, three times a week.

Crystals for Autism

People with autism are in a much higher vibration. They should carry Moldavite, Sugilite, Charoite or Sodalite crystals, put them under their pillow at night, or place them on their solar plexus.

Crystals for Cramps

Usually, cramps are caused by a lack of Calcium. Malachite, , Bloodstone, , Turquoise or , Chrysocolla can be used for all kinds of cramps   For menstrual cramps Chrysocolla works best.

Crystals for Migraines

Amethyst, Lapis Lazuli and Jet Crystal will help reduce or eliminate migraines. From my own experience place the crystals on your forehead when you have the first symptoms. Place the crystal also on the crown, the top of your head.

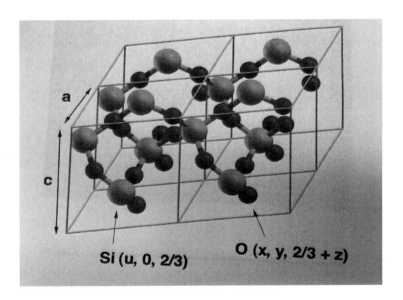

Si (u, 0, 2/3)   O (x, y, 2/3 + z)

Chapter 6

Techniques for Self-Healing (Part 3)

Restarting Your Immune System

Stimulating your immune system will give you instant energy and clarity, as well as open your paranasal sinuses. We are going to be working with the thymus gland, which sits in the upper part of your breastbone, otherwise known as the sternum, and it is a pinkish gray organ. The thymus gland is largest during puberty, after which time it slowly shrinks as we get older. It is the master gland of our immune system, and is what keeps our body strong and fights infections. The thymus produces white blood cells called the lymphocytes or killer T-cells.

As these T-cells circulate the bloodstream, they seek out viruses and destroy them. But the thymus is also involved with the endocrine system. The endocrine glands release hormones into the bloodstream, and those hormones travel to the cells and other parts of the body.

The thymus controls both growth and development where organs work on metabolism in a reproductive way, and helps to regulate your static system.

That is the same static system that helps protect your body against illness causing germs, bacteria, viruses and fungi. The thymus removes these from the system and also removes excessive fluid from the body tissues to help get rid of waste and toxins, together with all the obstacles that we are facing right now worldwide. What can we do naturally to build our immune system?

Besides eating properly, with this technique there is a fast and simple way to boost your immune system, but there's one thing that you should know before doing this technique. Do not do it before you go to bed because it will bump up your energy and it can affect your sleep.

Take your one finger, put it on top of the sternum bone, and you will feel a little indentation. Now take three or four fingers on your hand.

We're going to go to tap pretty much an inch below your indentation. You will get some adrenaline response because you're also going to get a nasal constriction in the paranasal sinuses and energy. But you're going to feel changes after you finish tapping, and you are going to get lots of energy.

You feel something has come over you. Understand that this is involved with your endocrine system. There are a lot of systems that are connected, as well as your central nervous system, so many people say well, I can breathe better now, so any change is good.

Take three of your fingers and go right over that bony area 3 inches below your throat. Start tapping about 20 to 30 seconds just to make sure you feel the response, and just keep tapping. You will experience changes.

You might feel a surge of energy going through your forehead, so just keep tapping. It is very effective, and very powerful for the nervous system after 20 to 30 seconds. When you're done, just sit and relax. You will feel changes come over you.

So, I challenge you, try tapping first thing in the morning. You will feel that surge of energy, your day will be much more productive, and you will build up your immune system, and this will help all your bodily systems to keep you strong and healthy.

If You Have Panic Attacks

Place Rhodonite, Kunzite, Turquoise or Sodalite crystals on your solar plexus and heart, and it will calm you down. You can also just hold them.

Chapter 7

Techniques for Self-Healing (Part 4)

Blue Lace Agate

Astro Signs: Gemini, -Pisces
Chakras: hroat, -Third Eye
Properties: Communication, Stabilizing, Calming

Blue Lace Agate is a stone of communication, helping those who have difficulty being heard by others, or who need confidence and articulation to share their truths. It provides clarity of thought and unwavering intent regarding what matters most.

What are the healing properties of Agate?

It transforms negativity into positivity. Agate enhances mental function, improves concentration, and enhances perception and analytical abilities. It is a soothing and calming gemstone that heals inner anger and anxiety, and helps in the strengthening of relationships. Agate instills security and safety.

What are Agate stones used for?

Industrial uses of Agate exploit its hardness, its ability to retain a highly polished surface finish, and its resistance to chemical attack. It has traditionally been used to make knife-edge bearings for laboratory balances and precision pendulums, and sometimes to make mortars and pestles to crush and mix chemicals. Metaphysical properties claim: Keep the crystal close to you to feel its energy.

Amethyst

Astro Signs: Pisces, Virgo, Aquarius, Capricorn
Chakras: Third Eye, Crown
Properties: Protection, Purification, Spirituality

Is Amethyst considered a precious stone?

Gemstone Information. Amethyst is the purple variety of the Quartz mineral family, and is considered a semi-precious stone and a royal stone. In fact, it has been very popular since ancient times, when royal families set it into crowns and scepters. Egyptians and Romans also loved this purple variety of the Quartz, that was considered a precious stone just like Ruby.

What does Amethyst mean spiritually?

Amethyst is a stone of spiritual protection and purification, cleansing one's energy field of negative influences and attachments, and creating a resonant shield of spiritual light around the body. It acts as a barrier against lower energies, psychic attack, geopathic stress and unhealthy environments.

What does the Amethyst represent?

Amethyst represents nobility, elegance, luxury, quietness, solemnitude and power. In Western tradition, Amethyst was the warmest symbol. It stands for honesty, kindness, good luck, and calm—all at the same time.

Can you wear Amethyst every day?

There are many reasons why purple gemstone quartz is not suitable for daily wear. Instead, wear your Amethyst on Saturdays as it will prevent the ill effects of Saturday.

The best time of the day is evening. However, if it's your birthstone, then go ahead and wear it every day.

Anglesite

Astro Signs: Pisces
Chakras: Third Eye—Crown
Properties: Manifestation—Communication—Meditation

Anglesite promotes sensitivity, gentleness, relaxation, and tenderness. Use this crystal to enhance meditation and promote stillness. Anglesite facilitates contact with those who have transitioned (passed over) and aids in the channeling process. Anglesite helps you to stay grounded during communication with entities from worlds other than the earth plane. Its loving energy allows for open communication with respect to spiritual issues. Anglesite can help to manifest dreams into this reality.

CAUTION: Contains lead and sulfur. Do not grind dry or inhale dust. Do not use in elixirs. Wash hands after handling. Keep away from pets and children! Due to its low hardness and perfect cleavage, Anglesite is only very rarely cut as a gemstone and not suitable for use in jewelry.

Origin of name: according to the English Wikipedia entry, William Withering, an English scientist, discovered the mineral in the Parys Coppermine on the island of Anglesey in Wales and recognized it as a mineral species in 1783.

The German Wikipedia entry states that Antoine Grimaldi Monet, a French mine-inspector general, described the newly discovered mineral as "vitriol de plomb," lead sulfate, as early as 1779. Its final name Anglesite was coined by François Sulpice Beudant (1787–1850), a French mineralogist and physicist, in 1832. Anglesite is a common mineral that is found in oxidized lead deposits.

Aqua Aura Quartz

What is Aqua Aura Quartz good for?

Soothes and clears the throat chakra, aiding communication with both the physical and angelic realms. Relaxes the respiratory system, easing breathing in asthma sufferers. Often used to clear the aura, or subtle bodies.

In crystal healing, stones are assigned various properties, though healers have different ideas about which stones possess which properties. Amethyst, for example, is believed by some to be beneficial for the intestines; Green Aventurine helps the heart; Yellow Topaz provides mental clarity.

Flame Aura Quartz is formed by bonding clear natural quartz with an infusion of titanium and niobium. This creates a magical play of colors and permanently alters the metaphysical properties of the crystal. The result is a beautiful crystal ideal for display, spiritual development, or healing work.

Different Types of Healing Crystals

- Clear Quartz. This white crystal is considered a "master healer." It's said to amplify energy by absorbing, storing, releasing, and regulating it.

- Rose Quartz. Just as the color may suggest, this pink stone is all about love.

- Jasper

- Obsidian

- Citrine

- Turquoise

- Tiger's Eye

- Amethyst

Aquamarine

Astro Signs: Gemini, Pisces, Aries
Chakras: Heart, Thymus, Throat, Third Eye
Properties: Protection, Communication, Calms

Aquamarine—the sea water stone—has a very soothing energy. The beautiful Aquamarine is associated with March, and so becomes the birthstone of the astrological signs of Pisces (March 1 through 20) and some members of Aries (March 20 through April 20) as well as the Chinese zodiac's sign of the Ox.

Most of the aquamarine on the market today comes from Brazil, Madagascar, Sri Lanka, Pakistan, Colombia, India, Russia, and several other countries. The name Aquamarine means sea water, and Aquamarine, like the Emerald, is a variety of Beryl.

In its light blue-green shades, Aquamarine can be quite affordable, but the deeper blue color of Aquamarine can command high fees. Most Aquamarine used in high-end jewelry is heat-treated to deepen its blue color, but raw Aquamarine has the benefit of a more potent energy.

Just like the Emerald, Aquamarine has a 7.5 to 8 hardness on the Mohs scale, meaning it is relatively strong compared to other gems but can still be broken without much effort.

Aquamarine can also lose some of its color if exposed to strong sunlight for extended periods of time.

Properties

Energy-wise, the Aquamarine is ruled by the moon, and is infused with yin or feminine energy. In its healing and nourishing effects, the Aquamarine can be compared to the Moonstone. Because of its flowing, peaceful energy,

Aquamarine has a strong ability to help move, protect, and purify your own energy and thus aid emotional healing as well as deepen meditative states.

Aquamarine's tendency to bring a joyful sense of harmony is akin to that of the Turquoise stone, but the energy effects are a bit different. While Turquoise tends to bring an earthy sense of harmony, Aquamarine shares its harmonious joy in a quite different manner. Its energy can feel like splashes of fresh ocean water—playful and a bit mischievous, too!

Aquamarine also does the following:

- Heals emotional trauma

- Cools high temper and conflict

- Relieves stress

- Helps get in touch with suppressed emotions

- Brings peace

- Clears the mind

- Calms the heart

- Helps speak the truth, —Strengthens psychic abilities

Azurite

Astro signs: Aquarius, Sagittarius
Chakras: Throat, Third Eye, Crown
Properties: Communication, Intuition, Guidance

Azurite in shades of indigo combines the intuition of the violet ray with the trust of the pure blue ray. It brings wisdom, truth, dignity, and spiritual mastery. A stone of judgment and long life, it promotes introspection and can result in profound wisdom when used well.

A highly sought-after crystal in the world of gemstones, Azurite is known for its stunning blue color, which evolved over the millennia through reactions between copper, hydrogen, carbonate, and oxygen. Azurite features deep contrasting shades of blue, which comes from its fusion with Malachite, a closely related mineral that contains nearly the same chemistry. In crystal healing, Azurite enhances creativity and inner wisdom because it cleanses and activates the third eye chakra.

To channel the healing properties of Azurite, place it in your office or studio for a constant flow of its powerful energy. Because it stimulates creativity and enhances intuition, the Azurite stone is excellent for use as a study aid or during a work session in the studio. Before you begin work on a project, sit quietly with the stone for twenty minutes to benefit from its inspiring energy.

Borrowing from the Zen tradition of meditation, gaze at the stone and notice any thoughts or feelings that come up. Keep a notebook handy in case you want to write down any notes that would be helpful later. Then, gently let those thoughts and feelings fade away and begin to breathe rhythmically while being mindful of inhaling positivity and exhaling any negative thought patterns that are holding you back from your natural state.

Azurite-Malachite Metaphysical Properties

Azurite, sometimes called a "stone of heaven," is commonly believed to provide insight into all areas of life, promote intuition, stimulate creativity, dissolve impediments, and soften cold intellectualism with love and compassion.

Beryl

Beryl is a mineral composed of beryllium aluminum cyclosilicate. Well-known varieties of Beryl include Emerald and Aquamarine. Naturally occurring, hexagonal crystals of Beryl can be up to several meters in size, but terminated crystals are relatively rare.

What does Beryl symbolize?

Beryl has been said to have the power to keep demons away, to promote happiness and marital love, increase sincerity, cure laziness, protect travelers from danger, and maintain youthfulness. Pliny The Elder used a powdered form of Beryl to cure eye injuries, as well as disorders of the heart and spine.

How much is Beryl worth?

Pale yellows and yellow greens don't see high demand. Stones up to 10 carats with richer colors retail for up to $150 per carat, while those 10 carats or larger could fetch up to $265 per carat. Gems with greater clarity can also command higher prices. Our gem price guide has values for all Beryl varieties.

Is Ruby a Beryl?

Material colored by iron is almost always too light to be called Emerald, and usually lacks the distinct green color typically associated with Emerald. Emerald is the most popular and valuable variety of Beryl. Emerald, Sapphire, and Ruby are the "big three" colored stones.

Is Red Beryl valuable?

Red Beryl is estimated to be worth 1,000 times more than gold by weight, and is so rare that only one crystal is found for every 150,000 diamonds that are mined.

Beryl and Physical Health

Beryl has a detoxifying and liver stimulating effect. Also, it has a balancing effect on the nervous system. It helps with short sightedness and any symptoms typical of constant stress.

Beryl aids the organs of elimination. It strengthens the pulmonary and circulatory systems. It increases resistance to toxins and pollutants. It treats the liver, heart, stomach, and spine. It also aids concussion. Beryl crystal water will help throat infections if gargled. Beryl soothes after long term healing and emotional release work. It supports women during menopause.

Chapter 8

Techniques for Self-Healing (Part 5)

Black Onyx

Astro Signs: Leo, Capricorn
Chakra: Root
Properties: Protections, Strength

The Enigmatic Tales & Symbolism of Black Onyx

The Chinese also believed in the power of this stone, as Black Onyx is considered very protective and grounding for its holder. It is used especially in Feng Shui. This precious stone is known for the energy of strong support, stamina, and determination to help one persevere.

What are the healing properties of Onyx?

Onyx gives strength. It promotes vigor, steadfastness, and stamina. It imparts self-confidence, helping you to be at ease in your surroundings. Onyx banishes grief, enhances self-control, and stimulates the power of wise decision-making.

Misfortune and Onyx Symbolism

In fact, Onyx symbolism is replete with connections to bad luck. In Arabic, Black Onyx is known as "el jaza," which means "sadness." A manuscript from 1875 notes that, in China, slaves and menial servants mined Onyx.

What are the benefits of Black Onyx stone?

Black Onyx is a protection stone. Its purpose is to help prevent the drain of personal energy while at the same time absorbing and transforming negative energy.

How can I tell if my Black Onyx is real?

If you are serious about finding out if your Onyx is real or fake, you can put the stone through a scratch test or a fire test. Use a lighter to light the stone for 10 seconds before dropping it in water. If it is a real Onyx, the stone will remain unharmed, but if it's fake it will be melted.

How do you wear an Onyx stone?

Onyx gemstone should be put in silver on the last finger of the working hand. Onyx should touch the skin of your finger. While wearing Onyx recite the Mantra - "Om Bhum Budhaaya Namaha." Benefits: - Onyx stone enhances strength, stamina, durability, and self-control.

Bloodstone

Astro Signs: Aries, Libra, Pisces
Chakras: Root, Sacral, Solar Plexus, Heart
Properties: Detoxifying, Healing, Grounding

A stone of courage, purification, and noble sacrifice, the Bloodstone has a long history of use for its healing properties. It was considered a somewhat magical stone because of its ability to transmute negative energy and purify a space while protecting it at the same time.

Healing with Bloodstone

Bloodstone is an excellent blood cleanser and a powerful healing stone. It heightens intuition and increases creativity. It is grounding and protecting. Bloodstone draws off negative environmental energy, helping to overcome influences such as geopathic or electromagnetic stress.

What is Bloodstone used for?

Bloodstone is a powerful healing stone, used for thousands of years for its healing properties. It is often used to purify and detoxify the body. Great at grounding negative energy and cleansing the body, Bloodstone brings love into any situation and helps ground the negative energies surrounding that issue.

Where do you place a Bloodstone in your house?

Placed on the heart chakra, Bloodstone balances and grounds the heart energies. For Gaia healing, Bloodstone may be placed in an area of disturbed Earth energy. Wear it around your neck. It is particularly beneficial to wear a Bloodstone necklace so that it touches your skin. If Bloodstone is worn over clothing and not touching the skin, it will take much longer to work. This is due to the unique way in which Bloodstone works.

Blue Apatite

Astro Signs: Gemini, Libra
Chakras: Throat, Third Ey
Properties: Clarity, Spirituality, -Expression

Blue Apatite opens the throat chakra. It enhances communication in groups and facilitates public speaking. It heals the heart and emotions. Blue Apatite connects to an extremely high level of spiritual guidance.

What is Blue Apatite good for?

Blue Apatite encourages the formation of new cells and aids in the absorption of calcium. It helps heal bones and teeth, repairs cartilage, and is useful in the treatments for rickets, joint problems, arthritis, and motor skills. Blue Apatite may be used to soothe headaches and help with vertigo or dizziness.

What is the most important use of Apatite?

The primary use of Apatite is in the manufacture of fertilizer – it is a source of phosphorus. It is occasionally used as a gemstone. Green and blue varieties, in finely divided form, are pigments with excellent covering power.

What is Apatite known for?

Apatite is best known for its use as an index mineral with a hardness of 5 in the Mohs hardness scale. It is usually green in color, but can be yellow, brown, blue, purple, pink, or colorless. These colors are often so vivid that Apatite has frequently been cut as a gemstone. Apatite is a brittle material.

How much does Apatite cost?

Apatite usually sells for $700 to $ 20,000 per carat and above.

What is Blue Apatite good for?

Blue Apatite encourages the formation of new cells and aids in the absorption of calcium. It helps heal bones and teeth, repairs cartilage, and is useful in the treatments for rickets, joint problems, arthritis, and motor skills. Blue Apatite may be used to soothe headaches and help with vertigo or dizziness.

Blue Calcite

Astro Signs: Pisces, Cancer
Chakras: Third Eye, Throat
Properties: Soothing, Release, Communication

Blue Calcite is a gentle stone that invokes a calm, serene energy. It assists to lessen our anxieties and relax our frayed nerves. Aligned with our throat chakra, Blue Calcite encourages us to communicate in a peaceful, clear tone.

Blue Calcite is an enormously powerful stone when it comes to soothing and relaxing the emotional body. This stone is known to calm emotions and offers mental and etheric protection. Blue Calcite has many beneficial effects for anyone who suffers from anxiety or depression.

Some of the most popular properties of calcite are as follows:

Helps with emotional healing. Blue Calcite is also a good stone to use to grid your home or workplace, as it has a protective quality that may prevent theft. It can be useful to put a piece of Blue Calcite near to any areas where a thief might choose to gain access to your home or business. Calcite, which comes in dozens of colors, is a form of calcium carbonate, which is the mineral that makes up chalk.

While its name comes from the German word calcite (meaning limestone) and only came into use relatively recently, in the ancient world, Calcite was grouped together with gypsum and called "alabaster" for its fair, milky color. The largest piece ever found was discovered in Iceland, but Calcite is found all over the world.

"Stone of Inspiration"

Blue Calcite is the stone of inspirational vibrations, emitting subtle waves of pure creative energy. It has been known to project itself into the conscious mind in the form of a muse. This is how Blue Calcite can stimulate the throat chakra, which is the sacred center of our creative expression.

Blue Topaz

Astro Signs: Sagittarius, Virgo
Chakras: Thymus, Throat, Third Eye
Properties: Removes negativity, Support, Expression

Jewel of Love

Often associated with loyalty and love, this gem represents eternal romance and friendship. Blue Topaz symbolizes honesty, clarity of feelings, and deep emotional attachment.

Concentration and Communication

Blue Topaz is an extremely important gem when it comes to mental prowess. This jewel, with its comforting blue color, is said to help channel our thoughts to promote concentration and perspective.

In some Hindi beliefs including Vedic astrology, Blue Topaz is significant in helping spiritualists focus and meditate on important matters. Wearing Topaz may also help in making one an effective communicator. Delivering speeches, pitching an idea, or expressing your emotions are believed to be aided with this beautiful gemstone.

What does Blue Topaz symbolize?

The Blue Topaz gemstone symbolizes love as well as fidelity. Blue Topaz originates from the old Sanskrit 'Tapas,' meaning fire. This light blue transparent rock was named because of its power to cool hot water.

Blue Tourmaline

Astro Signs: Taurus, Libra, Scorpio
Chakras: Throat, Third Eye
Properties: Honesty, Compassion, Intuition

In the metaphysical world, Blue Tourmaline is a crystal of Spirit and peace, providing for deep meditation and bringing past hurts to the surface for healing. It encourages the release of emotional bonds and frees the mind to explore a higher consciousness and spiritual connection.

Can Tourmaline be blue?

Blue Tourmaline is also known as Indicolite, which is a variation of Indigolite. The name refers to its color of deep and beautiful blue. It's rarer than other Tourmaline crystals, and it's formed in shades of pale to dark blue. Some even exhibit a tinge of turquoise. BrazilianTourmaline is an intense blue to blue green stone.

The amazing world of Tourmaline

Most people consider Tourmaline to be a single mineral. But in fact, it is a group named for several different but closely related minerals. Members of the Tourmaline group are favorites among mineral collectors. Their rich and varied colors can captivate the eye.

Even the black opaque Tourmalines can shine nicely and produce sharp crystal forms. Tourmalines are cut as precious gems, carved into figurines, cut as cabochons, sliced into cross-sections and natural specimens are enthusiastically added to many crystal collections.

There are many unique properties of Tourmalines. Although the two most important properties which determine whether the stone that you have is Tourmaline are as follows:

Firstly, they are piezoelectric, which means that when a crystal is heated or compressed (or vibrated) a different electrical charge will form at opposite ends of the crystal (an electrical potential). Conversely if an electrical potential is applied to the crystal, it will vibrate.

Secondly, they are pleochroic, which means that the crystal will look darker in color when viewed down the long axis of the crystal than when viewed from the side. This property goes beyond the idea that the crystal is just thicker in that direction. Even equally dimensioned crystals will demonstrate this trait.

Chapter 9

Techniques for Self-Healing (Part 6)

Citrine

What is Citrine good for?

Citrine contains a solar quality of energy; therefore, it is traditionally considered a good healing crystal for the solar plexus/third chakra issues. It can help strengthen self-esteem and a positive, vibrant flow of energy in and around one's body.

Citrine is a controversial crystal. Most of the Citrine on the market is actually heat-treated Amethyst, so when you buy a Citrine tumbled stone or a Citrine point you are probably buying a treated Amethyst.

It is not easy to recognize a genuine Citrine, but it is relatively easy to see if the so-called Citrine is a modified Amethyst. If the color of the citrine you are looking at is a deep, burnt orange-yellow, then it is best to keep looking for more sources to find your Citrine. A genuine Citrine is a gentle yellow color, and it is relatively rare.

Also known as the "Light Maker," the Citrine crystal has a bright yellow hue, which reflects its equally vibrant energy. Like Vitamin C for the soul, the Citrine crystal properties emanate positivity and joy. By connecting with Citrine, you can harness the energy of light and the energy of the sun embodied within this stone, which acts as a source of positive energy in all aspects of your life. From your attitude and outlook to your projects and pursuits, the Citrine crystal healing properties are perfectly suited to raise your vibration and help you embrace positivity and optimism as you move through life.

History & Lore

Citrine's name is derived from the French word citron, meaning lemon due to its color. Citrine has long been remarked upon for its subtle, honeyed beauty. Though the stone has an abundant history of being used in jewelry by ancient civilizations, Citrine is actually very rare today. Most Citrine seen on the market is Amethyst that has been heat treated to achieve a yellow hue.

Real Citrine was used in the jewelry of Greek and Roman civilizations dating back to the 1st century A.D. Citrine was also featured in the flamingo brooch of the Duchess of Windsor and in the Bulgari Cerchi earrings. Known as "The Merchant's Stone," Citrine is said to bring prosperity when placed in a cash register.

Origin & Regionality

Citrine is found in Brazil, Madagascar, Russia, and the United States. Due to its association with the solar plexus chakra, the Citrine crystal is effective in increasing your personal power and self-confidence. Enhancing this energy center can help dissolve blocks and stagnation, resulting in higher energy levels and a boost in overall circulation. Citrine's bright and happy energy fills your spirit with positivity and the highest vibrations, clearing any blockages or imbalances in your solar plexus chakra with its sunny energy. This makes a Citrine crystal ideal for a variety of intentions, including happiness, confidence, manifestation, and wealth.

Choosing Happiness

One of the primary uses for a Citrine crystal is for an intention of happiness and positivity. The Citrine crystal uplifts your spirit and aligns your energy with its high vibe energy. Whether you tend to have a pessimistic or negative outlook on life, or you're going through a rough patch and need to shift your state, the bright and vibrant energy of your crystal will emit a higher frequency to stimulate feelings of optimism and positivity. It guides you out of the darkness and into the light.

How to Use Your Citrine Crystal for Manifesting Wealth

To manifest wealth and success, create a Citrine crystal program for yourself that includes wearing it, carrying it, and placing it in your space.

Wearing Citrine

For constant access to the bright and uplifting energy of this stone, you can wear Citrine jewelry. As soon as it meets your skin, the stone will bring opportunity and abundance into your life simply by elevating your sense of optimism. This boost of positivity allows you to keep your energy focused on manifesting your dreams, without letting negativity get in the way.

Carrying Citrine

To enhance your crystal manifestation practice, keep a piece of Citrine in your wallet, purse, or pocket to carry the energy of abundance with you wherever you go.

Placement of Citrine

To complete your crystal practice, place a Citrine crystal in your space. For manifesting wealth, we suggest placing it in your office, on your desk, or near your workspace. You could also place it on top of a business card or financial document to call in wealth and success.

Citrine Crystal Intention for Manifesting Wealth

When working with Citrine for attracting wealth, use the following crystal intention: "I manifest wealth, success, and abundance."

Copper

Astro Signs: Taurus, Sagittarius
Chakras: Root, Sacral
Properties: Grounding , Balance, Energy

Copper has long been used as a healing metal, especially for arthritis and rheumatism. Copper has been used with blood and metabolism disorders. Copper acts as a conductor when worn on the body. Copper will help the healing effect of any stone when both touch the body.

5 Health Benefits for Wearing Copper Bracelets

- Joint stiffness and joint pain. Thousands of people have felt relief and relaxation from joint problems, especially those with joint stiffness.

- Mineral absorption. A pure copper bracelet has micro minerals such as iron and zinc

- Increasing cardiovascular health

- Healthier immune system

- Anti-aging

Does Copper promote healing?

Copper destroys and inhibits the growth of microbes, fungi and bacteria, including E Coli. It can be used as medicine when ingested (from water stored in a copper vessel) or applied topically to boost your immune system, prevent infection, improve wound healing, and speed the healing process of tissues.

According to court documents, a 2012 Tommie Copper catalog claimed that, "Copper has been used for thousands of years to aid in reducing inflammation, growing and sustaining connective tissues and aiding in blood flow and oxygen transport," and that it "provides immediate relief from inflammation."

Copper bracelets and magnetic wrist straps have no real effect on pain and swelling in rheumatoid arthritis, a new study finds. They also seem to have no effect in preventing the disease from getting worse. The practice of wearing copper bracelets to help RA has been popular since the 1970s.

Emerald

Astro Signs: Taurus, Gemini, Aries
Chakras: Heart
Properties: Prosperity, Hope, Healing

What are Emerald crystals good for?

Emerald brings loyalty and provides for domestic bliss. It enhances unconditional love, unity and promotes friendship. It keeps partnerships in balance, and can signal unfaithfulness if it changes color. Emerald stimulates the *heart chakra*, having a healing effect on the emotions as well as the physical heart.

What is the spiritual meaning of Emerald?

Also called the "Stone of Successful Love," Emerald opens and nurtures the heart and the heart chakra. Its soothing energy provides healing to all levels of the being, bringing freshness and vitality to the spirit. A stone of inspiration and infinite patience, it embodies unity, compassion, and unconditional love.

Is Emerald a good luck stone?

The Emerald has been considered a valuable gemstone since the ancient times and worn by royalty. People of ancient times thought of emeralds as a promise of good luck, and to have healing properties or promoting good health. The Aztecs regarded the stone as holy.

Hackmanite

Astro Signs: Sagittarius
Chakras: Throat, Third Eye, Heart
Properties: Trust, Self Esteem, Spirituality

What is Hackmanite?

Hackmanite is a variety of Sodalite containing sulfur. It changes color in light and reverts when in the dark. As with other sodalites, Hackmanite has a strong clearing effect on both the physical and energetic body.

What is the Sodalite stone good for?

Sodalite brings emotional balance and calms panic attacks. It enhances self-esteem, self-acceptance, and self-trust. Sodalite balances the metabolism, boosts the immune system, and overcomes calcium deficiencies. It combats radiation damage by soaking up electromagnetic smog.

Why does Sodalite glow?

Specifically, the rock in question is partially composed of a mineral called Sodalite, which is a fluorescent mineral. Electromagnetic radiation (such as light from a UV flashlight) at one wavelength is absorbed by the mineral, which then re-emits radiation at a longer wavelength – in this case, the yellow glow.

Hackmanite has an extremely fine vibration while remaining connected to the Earth. Hackmanite can help to combine higher intuition with mind and logic. Hackmanite is a wonderful crystal to use when wanting to attain a deep, spiritual meditative state. It facilitates feelings of joy, freedom, and happiness.

Known as the chameleon crystal, Hackmanite contains what scientists call tenebrescence, which is the ability of a stone to change color when exposed to light. In this case, pink Hackmanite will turn colorless when in sunlight, and slowly return to its former pink when left in the dark.

Hackmanite helps to embrace the self, enhancing self-esteem and feelings of self-worth. Use Hackmanite when working with issues of trust, be it self-trust or trust of others. Hackmanite is a strong support crystal. Its lesson is to stay true to self, to stand up for what you believe without fear of judgment, guilt, or criticism. Hackmanite encourages full and complete expression.

Mentally, Hackmanite can help loose and release the bonds of rigid mindsets of the past and in its place create an opening/infusion of the mind, allowing an infinite number of new and exciting possibilities to fill the space.

Hackmanite can work in any area to clean and clear electromagnetic pollution/smog.

Hackmanite is wonderful healing tool. Physically it can help aid imbalance, support metabolism, strengthen the immune system and ease insomnia.

Science & Origin of Hackmanite

Hackmanite is a rare sulfur chloric sodium aluminum silicate member of the Sodalite family. It crystallizes in the form of masses, cubic and octahedral formations. This is one of the very few minerals that is tenebrescent (changes color when exposed to sunlight), as well as UV reflective. It can be seen in a variety of colors such as grey, green, yellow, violet, pink, and blue, but most found in a dusty white. Hackmanite was first discovered in Greenland by L.H. Borgstroem in 1901. He named it after the famed Finnish geologist, Victor Axel Hackman. Important deposits of Hackmanite are in Afghanistan, Myanmar, Canada, Norway, and Russia.

Halite

Astro Signs: Cancer, Pisces
Chakras: Heart, Sacral
Properties: Healing, Purification, Cleansing

Also known as Rock Salt, Halite comes from the Greek words halos, meaning "salt, sea" and lithos, meaning rock. A mineral of purification, Halite can cleanse the aura, deflect negativity, and balance the emotions—especially helpful for those who suffer from mood swings.

What is special about Halite?

Halite, commonly known as rock salt, is a type of salt, the mineral (natural) form of sodium chloride (Na Cl). Halite forms isometric crystals. It commonly occurs with other evaporite deposit minerals such as several of the sulfates, halides, and borates.

What Halite is used for?

Some of its most common uses are as food seasoning, for road safety to melt snow and ice, as salt licks for cattle (these provide the cattle with salt, which is essential to their health), and for medicinal purposes. Halite is also the most important ore of the elements sodium and chlorine.

Why is Halite not a gem?

Salts readily precipitate from and dissolve in water. Natural salts like Halite (NaCl) and gypsum ($CaSO_4$) are soft minerals (not suitable for gems because they scratch or fracture easily and can dissolve in water.

Historical Folklore

It is said that Halite's auric cleansing abilities are based on its color. For example, pale white Halite is thought to harness the power of the heart, removing obstructions that stand in the way of one's inner guidance, while pink Halite prevents spirit attachment.

Halite is thought to be excellent for detoxifying the body. It enhances the functions of the metabolism and intestines. This stone is also useful for strengthening cellular memory, skin cells, and the respiratory system.

Herkimer Diamond

Herkimer Quartz "Diamonds" are extremely popular outside the walls of Central New York. Believe it or not, Herkimer Diamonds are powerful amplifiers of spiritual energy. They are used for healing, and they are used in meditations, dream and vision work, and advanced spiritual work.

Herkimers rival true diamonds. A true diamond found in the rough is exactly that, a rough appearing glass-like stone. Herkimer Diamond quartz crystals falls at a 7.5 on the scale, giving the real diamond a close race. They are naturally faceted, each having eighteen facets and 2 points.

How do Herkimer Diamonds heal?

In crystal body layouts or healing grids, Herkimer Diamond creates some of the purest light frequencies available to the physical body. Placing a Herkimer on the body or on a chakra will allow exceptional light frequencies to permeate the area where it is placed.

Herkimer Diamond Chakra Healing and Balancing Energy: Herkimer Diamond, with its pure, crystal light, clears the chakras, opening channels for spiritual energy to flow. It stimulates conscious attunement to the highest level and is particularly helpful in activating and opening the crown and third eye chakras.

Water included Herkimers are one of the more helpful quartz formations or configurations for healing emotional problems, as they bring the crystal energy of the stone to the heart.

It is a blissful stone to use during meditation. The purity and beauty of the energy of these crystals may *draw angelic beings and higher spirit guides* to it. You may find that you start connecting to angels.

Herkimer Diamonds will attune to a person using them, and like most quartz crystals are known to be able to retain information. Use the energy of positive affirmations in combination with this crystal.

You might like to program it with a positive affirmation before going to sleep to create a positive attitude, or to wake up with a clearer mind-set.

Chapter 10

Techniques for Self-Healing (Part 7)

Records Are Written in Stone

Down through the ages, monuments have been erected and inscribed by men with various patterns of designs and decorations.   In this chapter we will discuss a deeper meaning to the stone structures. Let us now think of them as means of communication of information from past minds.

They may also be devices for amplifying weak energy fields that are contained in the soil caused by movement of the subterranean bodies of water and the accumulation of various minerals and elements. These subterranean forces have been given the name Leylines, and location and direction of these lines of force may be detected with the use of a pendulum held in one's hand or a pair of dowsing rods, moving subterranean fields when crossing in a positive direction give amplified signals at the crossover point.

When crossed in opposing or negative directions they give weakened or negative feel. Leylines occur in the right-handed and left-handed spiral information.

The direction of stones and stone monuments over these areas amplify these fields. They create a vortex of energy which are often called sacred spots.

One of these is Stonehenge. The pattern of energy which has been doused corresponds to the placement of stones that are at this site. The same appears for the great pyramid in Egypt. I actually took a trip to Visoko, Bosnia to see their pyramids that are almost 30,000 years old, and I sat on the top where the energy comes out into space. It felt amazing.

Creative Visualization

One important way of doing creative visualization to heal is by taking you back 20 years, and it depends what you're trying to accomplish. As an example, if you had kidney problems, one way of helping you with the crystal is to take you back when you were totally healthy 20 or 25 years ago. Work with the crystal, pointing it towards your thymus gland, and using pure love and intention, then pulse your breath in a loving way to join the current and old perfect kidney to eradicate the problem and try to feel it.

The Power of Love

When you generate an act of loving in your body, the field is created. This field is transferred by an act of will from the initiator to the recipient. We can look on love as glue that holds matter and form and has entered the element of consciousness and contains the program for the total well-being of an individual.

This is fully understood and manifested by Jesus Christ. When asked what the primary law was, he answered to love the Lord your God with all your heart with all your soul with all your strength and with all your mind, and love your neighbor as yourself. Working on strength with all your mind, which crystallizes crystals, facilitates the transfer of this charge generated by mind. This way it is totally harmless to the crystal, and will amplify the weak field we first generate as we release this field with intention and breath. The field moves like a laser into the energy or subtle body of the recipient.

Enlightenment

There are thousands of pages and books written on enlightenment. Enlightenment begins when you discover you can trust yourself and the divine power within you. All starts to happen as soon as you're able to let go of the limiting belief that tells you who you should be, and that anything worthwhile must be very difficult and complicated. And that you are not good enough or smart enough, or highly evolved enough to be worthy of receiving this most awesome knowledge.

Self-Healing With the Vogel Crystal

To release unwanted tension in your body, put the base of the crystal in your palm, and place your thumb and index finger on the top. Pulse your breath and look at the face of the crystal. Visualize the area in your body having discomfort. Create an image of your body being well and free of pain, and pulse your breath with intention on what you wish to accomplish. Pulse your breath in again and pick another face of the crystal and repeat the above operation. Now reverse the tips of the crystals so it points in the opposite direction and repeat the same operation.

his morning and night, and most simple pains will be eliminated. If not see your doctor.

Dioptase

Astro Signs: Scorpio, Sagittarius
Chakras: Heart
Properties: Healing, Prosperity, Stress Relief

Dioptase is a translucent crystal colored by copper deposits, which give it an intense emerald or blue-green color.

Dioptase Stone Healing Properties

Besides providing you with emotional healing, this stone can also help you physically. It is useful in providing you with proper care and treatment of cardiovascular disorders. It helps in the detoxification of blood and treatment of blood disorders. It is also of help in treating disorders of the central nervous system, and helps you to strengthen your physical heart. It is helpful in treating headaches and migraines, lung disorders, respiratory problems, in fortifying female reproductive system and easing premenstrual syndrome. It also helps to strengthen your bones and teeth.

Dioptase Special Properties, Uses & Benefits

This is a very special stone which has many uses. Besides providing you with emotional healing, it can also be used in the treatment of many diseases related to different parts of your body like stomach, ulcer, respiratory system, and reproductive system. It has been used since the ancient world for its beautiful color – the first known usage of dioptase was on a statue dating back to 7200 years BC.

Dioptase occurs in copper mines and natural copper deposits, where the large quantities of copper ore in the ground become trapped in the silicate matrix of the crystal (which is essentially a form of quartz). They are fragile stones and should be handled delicately to prevent splitting. The only reason why they have not flooded the market – their color makes them seem very similar to emeralds, and if they were a little hardier, they would make wonderful replacements.

The first deposits of Dioptase found in the modern world were discovered in Kazakhstan in the eighteenth century.

The miners were very disappointed when they realized that what they'd discovered wasn't an emerald mine!

Deposits are found mostly in desert regions with high quantities of copper in the soil. It is an uncommon mineral, so if you are lucky enough to acquire a piece of Dioptase, you should treasure it and handle it with care!

Sources

For Chapters 4 through 9, I used concepts from Crystal Guidance as a source of inspiration, but restated some of the wording.

In Chapter 7, concerning techniques for self-healing, some of the ideas came from the Healing Crystals Database—Healthline and others of the Web, along with my own personal knowledge and experience.

Made in United States
North Haven, CT
28 November 2021

11520988R00050